REASONS TO BE PRETTY

"Mr. LaBute is writing some of the freshest and most illuminating American dialogue to be heard anywhere these days . . . *Reasons* flows with the compelling naturalness of overheard conversation. . . . It's never easy to say what you mean, or to know what you mean to begin with. With a delicacy that belies its crude vocabulary, *Reasons to be Pretty* celebrates the everyday heroism in the struggle to find out." —**Ben Brantley**, *The New York Times*

"There is no doubt that LaBute knows how to hold an audience. . . . LaBute proves just as interesting writing about human decency as when he is writing about the darker urgings of the human heart." —**Charles Spencer**, *Telegraph*

"Funny, daring, thought-provoking . . ." —**Sarah Hemming**, *Financial Times*

IN A DARK DARK HOUSE

"Refreshingly reminds us . . . that [LaBute's] talents go beyond glibly vicious storytelling and extend into thoughtful analyses of a world rotten with original sin." —**Ben Brantley**, *The New York Times*

"LaBute takes us to shadowy places we don't like to talk about, sometimes even to think about . . ." —**Erin McClam**, Newsday

WRECKS

"Superb and subversive . . . A masterly attempt to shed light on the ways in which we manufacture our own darkness. It offers us the kind of illumination that Tom Stoppard has called 'what's left of God's purpose when you take away God.'" —**John Lahr**, *The New Yorker*

"A tasty morsel of a play . . . The profound empathy that has always informed LaBute's work, even at its most stringent, is expressed more directly and urgently than ever here." —**Elysa Gardner**, *USA Today*

"*Wrecks* is bound to be identified by its shock value. But it must also be cherished for the moment-by-moment pleasure of its masterly portraiture. There is not an extraneous syllable in LaBute's enormously moving love story." —**Linda Winer**, *Newsday*

FAT PIG

"The most emotionally engaging and unsettling of Mr. LaBute's plays since *bash* . . . A serious step forward for a playwright who has always been most comfortable with judgmental distance." —**Ben Brantley**, *The New York Times*

"One of Neil LaBute's subtler efforts . . . Demonstrates a warmth and compassion for its characters missing in many of LaBute's previous works [and] balances black humor and social commentary in a . . . beautifully written, hilarious . . . dissection of how societal pressures affect relationships [that] is astute and up-to-the-minute relevant."   —**Frank Scheck**, *New York Post*

THE DISTANCE FROM HERE

"LaBute gets inside the emptiness of American culture, the masquerade, and the evil of neglect. *The Distance From Here*, it seems to me, is a new title to be added to the short list of important contemporary plays."

—**John Lahr**, *The New Yorker*

THE MERCY SEAT

"Though set in the cold, gray light of morning in a downtown loft with inescapable views of the vacuum left by the twin towers, *The Mercy Seat* really occurs in one of those feverish nights of the soul in which men and women lock in vicious sexual combat, as in Strindberg's *Dance of Death* and Edward Albee's *Who's Afraid of Virginia Woolf.*"   —**Ben Brantley**, *The New York Times*

"A powerful drama . . . LaBute shows a true master's hand in gliding us amid the shoals and reefs of a mined relationship." —**Donald Lyons**, *New York Post*

THE SHAPE OF THINGS

"LaBute . . . continues to probe the fascinating dark side of individualism . . . [His] great gift is to live in and to chronicle that murky area of not-knowing, which mankind spends much of its waking life denying."

—**John Lahr**, *The New Yorker*

"LaBute is the first dramatist since David Mamet and Sam Shepard—since Edward Albee, actually—to mix sympathy and savagery, pathos and power."

—**Donald Lyons**, *New York Post*

"*Shape* . . . is LaBute's thesis on extreme feminine wiles, as well as a disquisition on how far an artist . . . can go in the name of art . . . Like a chiropractor of the soul, LaBute is looking for realignment, listening for a crack." —**John Istel**, *Elle*

BASH

"The three stories in *bash* are correspondingly all, in different ways, about the power instinct, about the animalistic urge for control. In rendering these narratives, Mr. LaBute shows not only a merciless ear for contemporary speech but also a poet's sense of recurring, slyly graduated imagery . . . darkly engrossing."

—**Ben Brantley**, *The New York Times*

PHOTO: AARON ECKHART

NEIL LABUTE is an award-winning playwright, filmmaker, and screen-writer. His plays include: *bash*, *The Shape of Things*, *The Distance From Here*, *The Mercy Seat*, *Fat Pig* (Olivier Award nominated for Best Comedy), *Some Girl(s)*, *Reasons to be Pretty* (Tony Award nominated for Best Play), *In a Forest, Dark and Deep*, a new adaptation of *Miss Julie*, and *Reasons to be Happy*. He is also the author of *Seconds of Pleasure*, a collection of short fiction, and a 2013 recipient of a Literature Award from the American Academy of Arts and Letters.

Neil LaBute's films include *In the Company of Men* (New York Critics' Circle Award for Best First Feature and the Filmmaker Trophy at the Sundance Film Festival), *Your Friends and Neighbors*, *Nurse Betty*, *Possession*, *The Shape of Things*, *Lakeview Terrace*, *Death at a Funeral*, *Some Velvet Morning*, *Ten x Ten*, and *Dirty Weekend*.

WØYZECK

A PLAY BY GEØRG BÜCHNER

ADAPTED BY NEIL LABUTE

THE OVERLOOK PRESS
NEW YORK, NY

for werner herzog and klaus kinski

"we have it in our power to begin the world over again . . ."
—thomas paine

"yesterday, upon the stair, I met a man who wasn't there . . ."
—hughes mearns

"i dreamed about killing you again last night . . ."
—jeff tweedy

CØNTENTS

PREFACE

Remember when you were a kid and you used to search for hidden treasure? Sure you do. If you don't, I'm sorry for you—your childhood may have been even worse than mine and therefore I want to spend no time imagining it. For those intrepid explorers like myself, however, the idea of finding an old map or pots of gold or sunken pirate booty was a seminal part of our youth and, for me at least, one of the touchstones of my still fertile imagination (even if the odds of this happening in rural Washington State were probably extremely low).

As a reader, audience member and particularly as a dramatist, I believe *Woyzeck* represents one such pile of treasure. An unfinished text by Georg Büchner from the nineteenth century has given rise to many different versions—some compiled in varying arrangements of the existing scenes and even a few with entirely new material imagined for it (whether Herr Büchner likes the idea or not). I am one of those people, in fact, who has come to the text with ideas about the characters, the scenes and especially the ending. I have studied various translations and adaptations, along with the personal papers, lectures and letters of the playwright, which I've used as dialogue along the way for the character of "Woyzeck." I have re-imagined the entire setting of the play to one major location upon which the action plays out, and I've added one or two scenes at least that don't exist in any other version that I'm aware of, along with an ending that shifts the focus from the specific plight of the poor soldier Woyzeck to the wider political context of those with power and those without. The story goes that Büchner based his play on a true event from the day—perhaps one of

the first works to be "ripped from the headlines" like so many Hollywood films of yesterday and even today. In actuality, I don't really
care; Büchner has devised a timeless tale and one that will continue
to be read and performed for many years to come, be it in its original
form or featuring the music of Tom Waits or played with by drama-
tists like Robert Wilson or myself or others who will undoubtedly
follow. In the end, I choose a story to tell—I'm not much interested in
reality. I don't care if a thing is "probable" so much as is it "possible."
That's the world that I prefer to create within: the realm of possibility.

I've adapted a few different texts for both stage and screen, and
I must say that this one has been the most intriguing and mystifying
along the way. Part of that mystery will always lie in what isn't there;
I will forever wonder what Büchner would have done with the play
had he been able to finish it before his death (at the tender age of 23,
as well, which is sobering when one considers just how much he
achieved in his relatively few years on Earth). Would his ending have
been anything like mine? Who knows and, frankly, who cares? I've
had too many playwriting teachers along my path who tried to instill
their own rules of writing onto my process, and I've learned virtually
nothing from them, other than how they might have written one of
my plays. This was both useless and time-consuming. In fact, I've
come to the conclusion that playwriting cannot be taught but it can
be learned—sadly, this realization came after spending many years
teaching playwriting so there's a tasty bit of irony for you. The best
I can do (and I do try to do it with all my students) is to be a voice of
reason and insanity, to foster an environment of safety and chaos, to
create deadlines and problems for people so that they can find their
own trail up the mountain. Usually they want to believe that there is a
secret key that will unlock the gates to the path reserved especially
for "playwrights." I am happy to tell these writers that the secret key to
writing is that there is, in fact, no key. We all do it differently and thank
God for that. Everybody has a different process and I have learned
to not care what someone else does as long as they do it well. We
need more plays and films and television to watch. I can't write it
all—although I would be happy to try—and I appreciate the success
of others rather than despise it. Bad karma is bad karma and life is
already hard enough; I don't need a random bus to come along and

knock me down to remind me that this is not a race, it is not a com-
petition, and one must work against the American mindset of winning
all the time. If somebody else writes a great play, I'm the first one to
want to go enjoy it on stage. I may have a flash of envy because
I love to be working but more often than not I'll be the first to laugh
and clap and to say "Bravo!" at the end (well, maybe not "Bravo!"
because then people think you're pretentious, but you know what
I mean). I might not go up to them and congratulate them in person
as I'm a rather shy type by nature, but sometimes I'll find the courage
to at least give them a pat on the back or a handshake or even a
hug (if I've had a Diet Coke at the interval).

"Bravo!" is certainly what I would've said to Herr Büchner, however,
if I'd ever met him (although I don't speak German so I probably
would've just smiled and given him a "thumbs up" from across the
auditorium—this in itself is a fairly fanciful idea because *Woyzeck* was
never produced in his lifetime). I do remember reading the play as part
of a "Theatre History" course in college, and it was one of those pieces
that caused a good deal of discussion in class—about the setting and
the characters and the themes of the play. While many historians would
mark *Woyzeck* as at least an arguable starting point to the notion of
"Modern Drama," I was simply transfixed by the way that so many
scenes could gather steam and create a portrait of a society that was
heading toward disaster. The "haves" and "have nots" have always
existed (except maybe in the Garden of Eden, if you believe in that kind
of thing), and the historical figure of "Johann Christian Woyzeck" (and
the murder he committed) certainly seems to have served as both an
inspiration for Herr Büchner and as a primal scream for the "little guy"
everywhere (and maybe even the poster child for Edvard Munch's most
celebrated work). My ending has taken that idea to the next logical
place, actually; Woyzeck having finally made an impression on someone—his bunk mate Andres—who takes his call to violence literally and
begins to do just that. It might not be the last thing that Büchner himself
would've done, but fuck it, he's not here now and the pen is in my hand
for the time being. If someone comes along and adds a new ending to
Fat Pig or another few scenes to *The Shape of Things* after I'm gone, I
don't think I'll have too much to say about it.

Working on *Woyzeck* was the literary equivalent of a "blast" and

I will continue to explore the world of adaptations in any way I can or see fit. I want to keep pushing myself and this is a legitimate way to globetrot a bit without ever leaving the comfort of my own house (or apartment or tent or whatever it is I end up calling "home").

The short drama that accompanies *Woyzeck* here is an original piece that I wrote as a companion play specifically for this volume. I wanted to include a new bit of writing as well as this adaptation, and I pushed myself to create something using some very similar thematic elements to help create a kind of unified effect between the two. *Kandahar* evokes the same kind of soldier as *Woyzeck*, one who is lost in his sense of duty and devotion, both to the military and to a woman. I also wanted to embrace some of the recent incidents that have taken place on a variety of military bases in the United States without bogging it down in facts and sensationalized true events. The young veteran who haunts the interrogation room in this playlet is another in a series of dramatic snapshots that I've taken of modern man as he slowly struggles to evolve while sliding further and further back into the primordial ooze that has birthed him. In other words, I'm a guy and I often write about other guys because I know the great highs and catastrophic lows that we are capable of as members of that fragile fraternity known as "man."

As always, I've done my best. I hope it's good and I hope you'll like it. If you don't—or my adaptation of *Woyzeck*, for that matter—then you know where to find me. Actually that's just an expression since I really hope you have no idea where I live; after all, I don't know where you live (and I'm just fine with that).

And finally, I've dedicated this adaptation of *Woyzeck* to Werner Herzog and Klaus Kinski because their film version of the play was my first contact with the source material (even though, as previously mentioned, I went on to study the actual text in college). I watched their collective work with equal parts horror and fascination and many of their images remain vividly etched in my memory. Their film is a ferocious thing of beauty and if you haven't seen it, I suggest you immediately drop this volume on a nearby coffee table or night stand—it will keep, I assure you—and hurry to iTunes or your Netflix account and find their tantalizing take on this timeless tale. You will not be sorry.

WOYZECK

Woyzeck had its world premiere at Schauspielhaus Zürich in Switzerland in June 2006 as part of the "Zürcher Festspiele." It was directed by Wilfried Minks.

Woyzeck had its American premiere at the Ridge Theater at Virginia Tech University in November 2012. It was directed by Bob McGrath.

ENSEMBLE

KARL

WOYZECK

CAPTAIN

ANDRES

MARIE

MARGARET

DOCTOR

BARKER

DRUM-MAJOR

SERGEANT

JEW

STUDENTS

6 PATRONS

2 ATTENDANTS

GIRL IN STOCKINGS

TOWNSPEOPLE

VOICES

THE ØPERATING THEATER

Silence. Darkness.

Sound of a beer hall band in the distance. Distorted.

A match is struck, a face revealed. KARL (*the cripple*) *is leaning on crutches, a candle in one hand. Stares out toward the audience.*

KARL . . . once upon a time there was a poor little boy who had no mother or father. Everyone was dead and there was no one left in the whole world.

Lights up to reveal a nineteenth century operating theater. Row after row of seats towering off into the dark. At various intervals, faces of people staring out—our players, up to the rafters, waiting for their moment on stage.

(All action will take place in the rounded space between this onstage "audience" and the auditorium audience.)

Single light up slowly to reveal WOYZECK. *He sits alone on an upturned bedpan. Eating rapidly from a large bowl of peas.*

WOYZECK *reaches into his jacket and retrieves a little bundle. He looks about, then removes a tattered book and spectacles from the cloth.*

KARL Everything was quite dead. The boy was now completely alone, and he sat down and cried. He's sitting there . . . still.

KARL *smiles and crosses to* WOYZECK—*holds the light over* WOYZECK *as he begins to write haltingly. Reads aloud.*

WOYZECK ". . . if . . . anything can help in our time, then it is violence. Indeed, are we not . . . already in a constant state of violence?"

A sound in the dark. WOYZECK *looks nervously back over his shoulder. Nothing. He continues.*

WOYZECK "Because we were born and brought up in a prison . . . we no longer . . . notice that we are stuck in a . . . hole, chained by our hands and feet, with a gag in our mouths."

VOICES *cry out from the onstage spectators.* WOYZECK *looks up, startled.*

VOICES Woyzeck . . . Woyzeck . . . WOYZECK!!

WOYZECK "We do not have too much pain in this life, we have too little . . . Because through pain we arrive at God. We are death, dust, ashes . . . how should we complain?"

VOICES WOYZECK . . . WOYZECK . . . WOYZECK!!!

WOYZECK *hides his book and glasses away, taking up the bowl of peas again and eating feverishly.*

KARL *smiles and blows out the candle. Disappears. The sound of the band builds to a deafening roar.*

Blackout.

THE BARRACKS

WOYZECK *is shaving the* CAPTAIN, *who sits in a chair. Head back.*

CAPTAIN   . . . careful, Woyzeck. Be careful. One step after the
next. (*Beat.*) You make me nervous. What should I do with the
few moments you save rushing this way? What good will they
do me?

WOYZECK *steadies his shaking hand and forcibly slows down his
shaving. Takes a deep breath.*

CAPTAIN   Think, Woyzeck. Really think about this. You've got, what,
another thirty years left? Thirty good years. *Thirty.* (*Beat.*) You've
got to space it out, man! (*Beat.*) What else can you do with such
an *enormous* amount of time?

WOYZECK   Yes, sir.

CAPTAIN   I worry about the world, Woyzeck, the idea of eternity.
What is it? Eternity is eternity is eternity. Anyone can see that.
But it's also not that, not just that. Eternity. It's just one beat as
well . . . yes . . . just one single beat. It's rather horrifying, how life
turns about in a day. What a waste! And what does it all *mean*,
anyway? I can't bear to look at the miller's wheel any more, when
I pass it. I look away. It's too depressing.

WOYZECK   Yes, sir.

The CAPTAIN *is frustrated and shrugs off* WOYZECK *for a moment, studying him.* WOYZECK *waits at attention.*

CAPTAIN You always seem so frightened! Good people don't look like that, Woyzeck. Not a person with a clean conscience.

WOYZECK *nods, then returns to his shaving. The* CAPTAIN *eyes him suspiciously.*

CAPTAIN Say *something*, Woyzeck! What's the weather tonight?

WOYZECK Bad, sir. Very bad . . .

CAPTAIN Yes. It's an awful wind out there, isn't it? Gives me a chill. (*Slyly.*) I'd guess it's a North-Southerly . . .

WOYZECK Yes, sir.

CAPTAIN Ha! "North-Southerly!" Ha-ha! Lord but you're dense, Woyzeck! Awfully dense!!

WOYZECK *shudders and turns away. His hands begin to shake as he raises the razor up above his head. He stops as the* CAPTAIN *puts a hand on his shoulder.*

CAPTAIN You're a good sort, Woyzeck, but you're thick. And you've got no morals. Morals are, well, you know . . . when one observes morality. That's how it goes. But you've got a child without the blessing of the church. I believe that's the expression . . . "without blessing."

WOYZECK Being poor . . . the Lord has said to "suffer the little children that they should come unto him."

CAPTAIN What do you mean, Woyzeck? That's a strange thing to say . . . you're confusing the issue!

WOYZECK Don't you see, sir? Being poor . . . it's money. If you have no money, well . . . you're just barely getting along in this world. *Barely.* But we're flesh and blood, too . . . it's just that we never have any luck, that's all. Never. Here or in the hereafter. (*Beat.*) If I get up to Heaven, I expect I'll be put to work on the thunder . . . I'm sure I will.

The CAPTAIN *stares at* WOYZECK *—unsure how to deal with all that is spilling out of the man. The* CAPTAIN *stands up, shaving cream still on his face.*

CAPTAIN Woyzeck, you have no virtue. You are not the virtuous kind! "Flesh and blood?!" When I'm lying by the window, in my room, and it's been raining . . . if I see a pair of white stockings moving down the street, skipping down the . . . (*Beat.*) Well, damnit, Woyzeck, I feel desire, of *course* I do! I'm a *man*! But I'm a good man, Woyzeck. A virtuous man. And as they pass by, those stockings, I say to myself, "You're a good man, a virtuous man. A good, good man."

The CAPTAIN *stares at* WOYZECK *a moment, then settles back down into the chair. Closing his eyes.*

CAPTAIN And like all white stockings on sweet, thin legs . . . eventually, they move along.

WOYZECK *cautiously returns to the chore of shaving the* CAPTAIN*'s neck.*

WOYZECK Yes, sir, I think you're right, sir. I don't think virtue is much strong in me. You see, people like me, like us folks, we have little virtue. No use for it, really. We only have what's natural to us. To desire. Or want. (*Beat.*) But if I was a gentleman in a hat and coat with a lovely watch and all the proper words . . . I'd be virtuous, too. I know I would. It must feel wonderful, sir. To be virtuous. Problem is, I'm only a poor man . . . and no one wants to hear a poor man speak. Even when he has something to say . . .

CAPTAIN Look, Woyzeck, you seem like a good enough fellow . . . but you're always daydreaming. *Thinking.* (*Beat.*) You'll run yourself down, with all those thoughts of yours . . . you're wearing yourself out, with your grinding away on thoughts like those. You always seem so wrung out! (*Beat.*) You haven't been reading again, have you? . . .

WOYZECK Oh, no, sir . . . (*Looking around.*) Excuse me, sir, but I still have other duties to perform . . . wood to gather . . .

CAPTAIN Well, this discussion's upset me completely. (*Beat.*) Go along now, we're through . . .

WOYZECK *salutes, then drops the razor in a bowl.* WOYZECK *rushes off. Out into the street.*

CAPTAIN And no *running*! Go slowly down the street, Woyzeck. Nice and slowly . . . like a good fellow. With virtue.

As the CAPTAIN *wipes his face off with a towel, a young girl in white stockings crosses in front of the door to the barracks. Bouncing a ball.*

The CAPTAIN *watches her, then sits back and closes his eyes. Mumbling to himself.*

CAPTAIN . . . you're a good man. A virtuous man. A good, good man . . .

Blackout.

THE WØØDS

Thick, gloomy shadows all around. WOYZECK *is gathering firewood with* ANDRES, *who quietly whistles a tune.*

WOYZECK . . . this place is cursed, Andres, do you know that? Look, there, you see that stretch of grass over there? Where the toadstools are thick? A head—a man's head—rolls down it every evening. It does.

ANDRES *looks over at the spot, curious. Crosses to it.*

WOYZECK A person picked it up once. It's true, he did. Just picked it up. Mistook it for a hedgehog. Three days later, he was lying in his coffin.

ANDRES *stares over at him, uncertain. Finally, he smiles.*

WOYZECK It's true, Andres! I'm sure of it.

ANDRES *returns to picking up fallen branches. He whistles while he works.* WOYZECK *stands frozen on the spot.*

WOYZECK Listen! Hear it, Andres? Can you hear *that*? Something's moving . . .

ANDRES *stops and looks about. Worried.*

ANDRES The ground . . .
WOYZECK Yes! Moving beneath me, *behind* me.

WOYZECK *suddenly stomps up and down on the muddy earth. Gets down on his hands and knees.*

WOYZECK Listen! It's hollow, all hollow under there . . .

ANDRES It's frightening.

WOYZECK So strange . . . and still now. It takes away the breath.

WOYZECK *looks off into the gathering night. Staring.*

WOYZECK Andres!

ANDRES What, Woyzeck? What is it?!

WOYZECK Look, Andres! (*Beat.*) Look beyond the dark, above the town. It's glowing. A fire raging in the sky and a clamor below, as if . . .

WOYZECK *throws himself to the ground. He reaches up and pulls* ANDRES *down onto the muddy soil beside him.*

WOYZECK It's coming this way! Quick, don't look up, Andres!!

The sound of the band in the distance, building to a roar as the cries of "Woyzeck" follow. Then silence.

ANDRES Woyzeck? Is it gone?

WOYZECK Silence.

ANDRES I didn't hear . . .

WOYZECK Nothing but silence. (*Beat.*) As if the world had died . . .

ANDRES Listen, Woyzeck! We've got to get back . . . the drum is sounding!

Drums in the distance. ANDRES *stands and quickly gathers his bundles of wood.* WOYZECK *remains sitting in the mud.*

WOYZECK . . . as if it had *already* died.

Blackout.

THE ROOM

MARIE *sits near the window, holding her baby.* MARGARET *stands outside. The sound of the retreat being drummed.*

MARIE . . . ta-ra-ra! Hup-hup! Hear it, my dearest, my little one? Here they come . . .

The women watch as the DRUM-MAJOR *—straight and precise—comes marching down the street. Followed by others.*

MARGARET Look at that man . . . what a sight! Thick as a tree trunk . . .
MARIE . . . and strong as an ox, I'll bet.

The DRUM-MAJOR *gives the women a salute.* MARIE *smiles back at him.*

MARGARET My, that was an awfully friendly eye you gave him! You don't treat every man like that . . .
MARIE Soldiers are such handsome lads . . .
MARGARET Look at you! Your eyes are still gleaming!
MARIE What of it? (*Defiant.*) Perhaps you should take yours to the Jew and have him shine them, brighten them up for *buttons* and sell them . . .
MARGARET Who are you to talk like that? You with a baby in hand! (*Beat.*) *I'm* a good woman, that's what *I* am . . . but you've found your way inside many a pair of leather britches . . .

MARGARET *storms off with a basket of washing in hand.*

MARIE Bitch. (*Beat.*) Well, baby, let them have it however they wish.

It's true, besides . . . you're only a whore's child, you poor thing. But still, your little face fills my heart with so much joy.

MARIE *hums softly to the child.* WOYZECK *appears at the window. He knocks lightly.*

WOYZECK Marie . . .

MARIE Who's there? 'S that you, Franz?

WOYZECK Yes.

MARIE Come inside.

WOYZECK I can't. I've got to get back to the barracks.

MARIE Look at you, you're filthy! Have you been cutting wood for your Captain again?

WOYZECK Yes. In the forest . . .

Silence between them as WOYZECK *looks about, wide-eyed.*

MARIE What's the matter, Franz? You seem frightened . . .

WOYZECK There was something there again, Marie. Some *thing*, out there.

MARIE Now, now . . .

WOYZECK It followed us all the way back to town, Andres and me. It *pursued* us here. What does it mean?

MARIE Franz . . . where did you hear a word like that one? "Pursued?"

WOYZECK In a book of . . . (*Eyes her.*) Doesn't matter. I've got to go. I'll see you at the fair this evening. I can pick you up, if you like. I've put a little bit aside . . .

MARIE *smiles at him and nods. Reaches to touch his arm but he hurries off.*

MARIE Poor man! So haunted by everything in this world . . . didn't even stop to glance at his child. (*Beat.*) His thinking is so . . . his mind, wound like a clock spring! One day it'll break.

MARIE *shivers a bit and stands, moving to the window. She looks out.*

MARIE Why so quiet, my child? You're not frightened, are you? It's so dark out now, one could go blind and never know it. (*Beat.*) That lamp, the street lamp, usually shines in all night long, but tonight the shadows are drowning it out. (*Beat.*) It scares me . . .

MARIE *closes the window with a free hand and then moves off with the child.*

Blackout.

THE STREET

WOYZECK *leans against a wall, fastening up his fly. The* DOCTOR *moves to him and turns him roughly about.*

DOCTOR . . . what's all this, Woyzeck? Hmmm? (*Beat.*) I thought you were a man of your word.

WOYZECK What is it, Doctor?

DOCTOR I saw you, Woyzeck, just now. I saw what you did. Pissing in the street, like an animal on that wall!

The DOCTOR *removes two coins from a jacket pocket.*

DOCTOR And me, giving you two groschen a day . . . shall I throw them away? For all the good it does me! Shall I?!

The DOCTOR *throws the money into the mud.* WOYZECK *dives into the dirty water and searches madly about.*

DOCTOR It's bad, Woyzeck . . . the world, all of it, has turned rotten. Rotten to its core.

As WOYZECK *searches, the* DOCTOR *lashes him across the back with his walking cane.* WOYZECK *cowers.*

WOYZECK But Doctor, please! I have to relieve myself when nature calls!

DOCTOR Nature? Nature!! A man is *free*, Woyzeck. Man is the embodiment of choice. The *freedom* of choice. (*Beat.*) And you chose to deceive me!

WOYZECK But, Herr Doctor . . .

DOCTOR You deceived me, Woyzeck! That's what you've done . . .

The DOCTOR *reaches down and pulls* WOYZECK *to his feet.*

DOCTOR Have you eaten your peas, Woyzeck? You must eat *nothing* but peas! It is imperative . . . a revolution is beginning in science, and I must take my place! (*Beat.*) Uric acid 0.01, Ammonium hydroclorate, with hyperoxide . . . Woyzeck, can't you try again? Just once more? Let's go in and you can take a piss for me . . .

WOYZECK . . . I can't, Doctor . . .

DOCTOR But on a wall, though! And I have our agreement, in your very own handwriting! You wrote it down and I watched you do it . . . and then to find you out here, doing it against a stone wall. (*Beat.*) But listen, I'm not getting angry. Anger is not scientific, Woyzeck. No, see? I'm calm. Completely calm and relaxed. I have no reason to show my anger to you . . . you're just a man, after all. And barely even that . . .

WOYZECK But don't you see, Doctor? A man might be one sort of person, a certain type of person, but his *true* nature could be something else again. Another thing entirely. For example . . .

DOCTOR Woyzeck, stop! Stop now! You're *philosophizing* again so stop it!

WOYZECK Have you never seen the world from upside-down, Doctor? When the sky lights up with fire and it seems as if we'll all be drowned in flames? That's when the voices speak to me . . .

DOCTOR You're an aberration, Woyzeck.

WOYZECK It's my nature, Doctor. And when a man's nature is gone . . . well . . .

DOCTOR What do you mean, when his "nature is gone?" Hmm?

WOYZECK If one's nature goes, that's when all . . . is lost. When the Earth is so dark one has to feel his way about on hands and knees, until you're certain that it's all coming apart in your hands.

Even when there's something there—you can feel it—but yet there's nothing. (*Beat.*) Everything goes black, is darkness, and yet there's a glow in the West. Like a raging fire. When . . .

WOYZECK *stops, tries to concentrate. Can't. Starts to get worried.*

WOYZECK . . . it's getting late. Shadows.

WOYZECK *tries to back away but the* DOCTOR *stops him.*

DOCTOR You are such a beautiful specimen, Woyzeck. Of the second order . . . and fully formed, even! Lovely . . . second order . . . without hardly any impairment of faculties.

WOYZECK Yes, Herr Doctor.

DOCTOR Will you eat your peas?

WOYZECK Just as you say . . .

DOCTOR Continue to perform your duties?

WOYZECK Oh yes, Herr Doctor. Yes. I will.

WOYZECK *breaks free and then backs away, running off. The* DOCTOR *watches him go.*

DOCTOR You're such an interesting case, Woyzeck! (*To himself.*) Certain to become a patient in an asylum . . .

The DOCTOR *moves to the wet spot on the wall and fingers it lightly.*

DOCTOR . . . once I'm through with you, of course. After all, I must make my place. There's a revolution coming our way. *Pro-gress.*

The DOCTOR *removes a glove and scrapes at the moisture with an exposed finger.*

Blackout.

THE FAIRGRØUND

A ring of lights. Sawdust. Sound of a beer hall band in the distance.
KARL *leaning on his crutches. A boy dancing on barrels.*

WOYZECK *and* MARIE *enter, marveling at the booths. Other people milling about.*

WOYZECK . . . look at that poor little boy!

MARIE Yes.

WOYZECK Having to perform like that, it makes no sense . . .

MARIE Hmmm. When fools make sense, it'll make fools of us all.

WOYZECK . . . his face, joy and fear.

MARIE Oh, Franz, it's a crazy world . . . a crazy, beautiful world!

MARIE *swings the baby around in her arms, dancing. Happy.* WOYZECK *watches her for a moment, smiling. Pleased that she is pleased.*

Lights up on a BARKER *outside a dirty tent. A monkey on a leash sits next to him.*

BARKER . . . step up, ladies and gentlemen! Look at this creature, as God made him . . . he's nothing, absolutely nothing. Lowest form of animal life. But see now what art has done to him . . . yes, art!

The BARKER *cracks a whip and the monkey stands on its hind legs.*

BARKER Ah-ha! See how he walks upright like a man! How he wears a fancy jacket and trousers, even carries a sword! Look, he's no longer at the bottom of the food chain. Why, he's now a soldier!!

General applause from the gathered audience. WOYZECK *is now holding the child over his head, hoping for a better view.*

BARKER Come inside . . . see the little love birds . . . admire the astronomical horse . . . just one of the many wonders of Europe! It can tell any one of you your age, number of children, even your illnesses . . . yes, your illnesses! We've all got them, so why not *know* them? (*Beat.*) Show's about to begin, because we always begin at the beginning. Step in, step on in . . . step inside!

The BARKER *holds open the curtain, then he and the monkey disappear inside. A small crowd follows.*

WOYZECK Want to go in?

MARIE It's all the same . . . (*Beat.*) Yes, let's go inside . . . there must be wonderful things in there to see.

MARIE *waits while* WOYZECK, *baby in hand, goes off to one side to purchase tickets.*

The DRUM-MAJOR *and a* SERGEANT *arrive at the fair. The two men watch* MARIE *with an open hunger.*

SERGEANT Hold it . . . do you see that?

DRUM-MAJOR Yes. I've seen her before . . .

SERGEANT What a woman! Could breed a whole regiment of cavalry . . .

DRUM-MAJOR . . . or a battalion of drum-majors.

SERGEANT The way she holds her head. That flowing hair . . .

DRUM-MAJOR . . . and those eyes. Strange, dark. Like looking down a well . . .

SERGEANT . . . or up a chimney!

MARIE *glances over at the men as they laugh out loud. The* DRUM-MAJOR *moves to* MARIE, *offering an elbow. She glances at* WOYZECK, *then moves into the tent with the* DRUM-MAJOR.

WOYZECK *returns and looks around. The* SERGEANT *pats him on the shoulder.*

SERGEANT Looking for something, Private?

WOYZECK . . . Marie.

SERGEANT "Marie." hmmm . . . a beauty, with the red dress on?

WOYZECK Yes.

SERGEANT Wearing red, a girl all in red?

WOYZECK Yes . . .

SERGEANT Stunning face . . . in a bright red . . .

WOYZECK Yes, yes!

SERGEANT . . . haven't seen her.

WOYZECK *looks around the milling crowd, terrified. The baby starts to cry.*

WOYZECK Marie! (*Shouting.*) Marie!!

SERGEANT I'm joking, soldier . . . only joking. Of course I saw her. Can't miss eyes like those . . .

WOYZECK . . . but where?

SERGEANT Ran off toward the woods.

WOYZECK . . . the woods?

SERGEANT Looked over at you, she did. She looked and said something, but . . . ran off.

WOYZECK . . . off . . .

SERGEANT Probably to relieve herself. That would be my guess . . . to do it in the woods.

WOYZECK *stumbles off clutching the baby, screaming out "Marie!" The* SERGEANT *laughs and watches* WOYZECK *go off. He slips inside the tent.*

Blackout.

THE TENT

An old horse in the center of a circus ring. The BARKER *stands beside it, pointing at the crowd.*

MARIE *sits between the* DRUM-MAJOR *and the* SERGEANT. *Her eyes are gleaming.*

MARIE . . . the lights!

DRUM-MAJOR Yes. Like black cats with burning eyes . . .

SERGEANT What a night!

The BARKER *turns to the horse. Raises his hands up.*

BARKER Observe . . . the astronomical horse! Show us your talents! Your brute reason! Put these humans to shame! (*Beat.*) Ladies and gentlemen, this beast that stands before you—four hooves on the ground and a tail besides—is of a simple nature, but watch now and be amazed, my good fellows, as this nag applies logic to what is put before him. (*To the horse.*) Show them, horse! Show them what you do! (*Beat.*) I ask you now: are there any donkeys in the house? Out in the audience, are there any asses?

The horse shakes its head vigorously. The BARKER *claps.*

BARKER See the reasoning! He came, he saw, he nodded!! Remarkable . . . This is not merely an animal, this is a human being . . . well, at least a human animal!

The horse defecates at this moment, into the sawdust.

BARKER However, as you can see . . . he's still very *natural*. Not perfected, perhaps, but we can learn a lesson from him. Haven't we been told to be natural and return to nature? Aren't we all, each of us, risen from dust and sand and dung? We *are* dung, but dung that can reason! And so with this beast—ashes to ashes, dung to dung—natural but logical! Able to calculate, but with not a finger to count on. Therefore only an *animal* in your eyes, even as he is able to understand love, desire and all the rest . . . (*Beat.*) But how can he express himself, you ask? See for yourselves . . .

The BARKER *cracks his whip. Snap! The animal flinches.*

BARKER   Tell the audience what time it is! (*To the crowd.*) Ladies and gents, do any of you own a watch? A watch if you please!

The SERGEANT *stands and proudly pulls a gold watch from a pocket.*

SERGEANT   A watch? Will *this* do? . . .

Approval from the crowd; the BARKER *whistles loudly. The* SERGEANT *moves into the circle with the* BARKER *as* MARIE *bends forward to see better. The* DRUM-MAJOR *places a hand on her backside.*

MARIE   I don't want to miss this . . .
BARKER   Tell us the time, beast! (*Cracks his whip.*) Do it now!!
SERGEANT   This is *my* watch.
DRUM-MAJOR   . . . what a woman.

Blackout.

THE RØØM

MARIE *sits with a sleeping child in her lap, staring at herself in the mirror. She is wearing new earrings.* WOYZECK *asleep nearby.*

MARIE   . . . my, look how they dance in the light! What kind of stones did he say they were?

The child stirs in her arms—she soothes the baby softly.

MARIE   Go to sleep, my precious . . . close your little eyes. (*Beat.*) They must be gold. It's no matter that we have only a little corner of the world to live in, a fragment of broken glass in which to see . . . my lips are as red as the finest ladies with their mirrors from ceiling to floor, and lines of fine gentlemen waiting to kiss their hands . . . (*Studies herself.*) . . . and me, just a common thing.

WOYZECK *turns and sits up, startling her.* MARIE *jumps up, trying to cover her ears with a free hand.*

WOYZECK   . . . Marie. (*Beat.*) What have you got there?
MARIE   Nothing. Our child . . .

WOYZECK *studies her, moving slowly closer.* MARIE *keeps moving away from him.*

WOYZECK   I . . . lost you. At the fair. I was looking, but I couldn't find you. Not in the woods. (*Beat.*) I stayed with the boy . . . until . . .
MARIE   I . . . I was . . .

*She is now backed into a corner—*WOYZECK *continues.*

WOYZECK   . . . what is that you've got, Marie?

MARIE Where?

WOYZECK It's glowing. Through your fingers there.

MARIE . . . an earring. I . . . I found it.

WOYZECK Hmmmmm. I've never found that sort of thing before.
(*Points.*) Not *two* at a time . . .

MARIE So what? What are you trying to say?

WOYZECK Doesn't matter . . .

MARIE . . . I'm only flesh.

WOYZECK Look at the way the boy sleeps. Be careful there . . . lift
him up or you might hurt him. Look at his head, those drops on
his forehead . . . poor thing. Not even comfortable while he sleeps.
(*Beat.*) To us, *everything* is work.

MARIE *nods as* WOYZECK *studies her. A moment of silence, then the*
VOICES *rising up around them—only* WOYZECK *hears them.*

VOICES WOYZECK . . . WOYZECK . . . WOYZECK!!!

MARIE *keeps her eyes on* WOYZECK *as he looks around. He shakes his*
head.

MARIE . . . Franz? What is it?

WOYZECK *shakes again violently, then looks at* MARIE. *He puts one*
hand into his pocket and steps toward her again. She holds up her
free hand as protection.

WOYZECK *pulls a few coins from his pocket and places them in* MARIE'S
hand.

WOYZECK Didn't spend it all, Marie. My pay. Take it . . .

MARIE Oh, Franz . . . (*Relieved.*) You're very good to us. Too good.

WOYZECK Got to go. Goodbye, Marie . . .

WOYZECK *turns and exits quietly, leaving* MARIE *in a dark corner of the room. Looking around.*

MARIE   I'm such a horrid creature! Why don't I stab myself, cut my own throat?

MARIE *returns to the chair and sits, rocking the child.*

MARIE   Oh, what sort of world is this? It's going to hell, I'm sure of it. And us with it . . .

After a moment, she picks up the mirror and studies the earrings again. A slow smile.

Blackout.

THE ØPERATING THEATER

The DOCTOR *stands addressing a group of students.* WOYZECK *sits on a stool nearby.*

DOCTOR . . . Gentleman, observe! For three months this man has eaten nothing but peas . . .

WOYZECK Doctor, I've got the shakes . . .

DOCTOR Exactly! (*To* STUDENTS.) Please note the results. They're fairly obvious. (*Beat.*) An irregular pulse. Some uncontrollable movement in the limbs. And the eyes . . . do notice the eyes.

WOYZECK . . . it's all going black, Doctor.

A STUDENT *raises his hand. Stands.*

DOCTOR Yes, please?

STUDENT What is the patient's name, Herr Doctor?

DOCTOR He is called "Woyzeck." The first name escapes me . . .

Murmuring from the STUDENTS *—rising into the sound of many* VOICES.

VOICES WOYZECK . . . WOYZECK . . . WOYZECK!!!

WOYZECK *looks around, terrified—the* DOCTOR *notices none of this.* WOYZECK *covers his ears; the* DOCTOR *spots this and taps* WOYZECK *on the head with his cane.*

DOCTOR Courage, Woyzeck . . . this will all be finished in a matter of days. (*Beat.*) Oh, I've been meaning to show them . . . (*Smiling.*) Wiggle your ears for the young gentlemen, Woyzeck.

The DOCTOR *points to* WOYZECK'S *ears, grabbing one in each hand and pulling.* WOYZECK *grimaces.*

DOCTOR He uses two independent muscles. It's quite a trick . . .

WOYZECK Must I, Doctor?

DOCTOR Will I have to do it for you, man? They want to see it! (*To* STUDENTS.) Don't you?

The STUDENTS *nod and try to encourage* WOYZECK *by hitting their fists on their desks and calling out his name.*

VOICES WOYZECK . . . WOYZECK . . . WOYZECK!!!

WOYZECK *cringes at this, then complies. He stands up on the stool and turns in circles. The* DOCTOR *points with his cane.*

DOCTOR There! See, like a donkey he is! It's a case of reverse-evolution! The consequence of a female upbringing . . .

The DOCTOR *studies* WOYZECK'S *head as the* STUDENTS *watch.*

VOICES WOYZECK . . . WOYZECK . . . WOYZECK!!!

The DOCTOR *indicates that* WOYZECK *should continue turning up on his stool. The* STUDENTS *watch from their seats.*

DOCTOR You're losing your hair, Woyzeck. Have you been pulling on it again? Don't worry, man, it's only the peas . . . (*To his* STUDENTS.) Peas, gentlemen! Observe the creature, sustained by nothing but *peas*!! A revolutionary diet . . .

Blackout.

THE RØØM

MARIE *sitting up against the table, the* DRUM-MAJOR *with his face buried between the folds of her blouse.*

MARIE . . . oh . . . my . . . OH . . .

DRUM-MAJOR . . . GOD. Come on, Marie.

MARIE *stops him and forces him to stand, looking him over as he smiles at her. She brushes at his uniform.*

MARIE Show me again, first. How you do it . . . walk around the room.

The DRUM-MAJOR *nods and snaps to attention, strutting by her several times. Turning and doing it again.*

MARIE The chest of an ox . . . the hair of a lion . . . there's no one else like you. My God, you make me *proud* to be a woman!

DRUM-MAJOR Ha! You should see me Sundays with the plume on my helmet and a pair of white gloves . . . the Prince often remarks, "There goes a *real* man. Now that's a soldier for you!"

MARIE Oh, really? (*Teasing.*) A *real* man, huh?

DRUM-MAJOR He does indeed! (*Goes to her.*) And you're a real woman, Marie. I want to fill you with drum-majors. Set up a whole *stable* full of them . . . come on!

He goes to her, grabbing her by the wrist. It's almost playful, but a bit rough. MARIE *begins to struggle.*

MARIE No, let me go . . .

DRUM-MAJOR Come on, you wildcat.

MARIE No!

DRUM-MAJOR "No" becomes "Yes" if one waits long enough . . .

MARIE No!!

DRUM-MAJOR Yes . . . (*Smiles.*) I can see it, the devil in your eyes.

MARIE Don't touch me . . . no . . . no . . . (*Beat.*) . . . yes.

MARIE *is through fighting—she buries her mouth into his and they begin to kiss. Heavy. Hard.*

MARIE Oh, what does it matter? It's all the same . . .

Blackout.

THE STREET

The DOCTOR *walking down the street at a brisk pace. The* CAPTAIN *following behind him, calling out.*

CAPTAIN . . . Doctor! One moment, please. Why must we all be rushing about so? I don't understand it. All you'll do is rush to your death, Doctor . . . not the kind of thing a man with a clear conscience would do. Not at all.

The CAPTAIN *grabs the* DOCTOR *and holds him, even when the* DOCTOR *tries to pull away.*

DOCTOR I'm in a hurry, Captain. A hurry!

CAPTAIN But I need to speak with someone. I'm so down, Doctor. I feel like a man about to burst into tears . . . Even at the sight of my own coat hanging in the hall.

DOCTOR Hmmm . . . (*Stares at the* CAPTAIN.) Puffy. Fat. Thick neck. And subject to apoplexy, I'll wager. Yes, my dear Captain, you're headed for trouble soon enough. *Apoplexia cerebri.* Of course it may only affect one side or, with a bit of luck, it'll only attack the brain so that you will live on as some kind of vegetable. That's my prognosis, anyhow. I'll assure you, though, that if this is the case and the good Lord does decide to paralyze you . . . I will conduct experiments on you that will cause our names to go down in history . . .

The CAPTAIN *pushes the* DOCTOR *away, staggering back and off to one side.*

CAPTAIN Doctor, stop it now! You could kill a person from fright, you know . . . pure and simple fright! (*Beat.*) I can already imagine the mourners, using lemons to make the tears flow . . . Still, they'll say "He was a good man. A good, good man." (*Points at him.*) Ahhh, you're a damned ol' coffin-nail, you are!

The DOCTOR *smiles and tips his hat, turning away.* WOYZECK *suddenly appears, reading as he moves past. The* CAPTAIN *calls out.*

CAPTAIN Woyzeck! What's the hurry, man? Stop a bit . . .

WOYZECK *comes to a stop but doesn't turn to the* CAPTAIN *or the* DOCTOR. *Just stands there, fidgeting. Hides his book and glasses.*

DOCTOR What've you got there, Woyzeck?

WOYZECK Nnn . . . nothing, Herr Doctor.

CAPTAIN You rush around through the world like an open razor . . . you're going to give someone a nasty cut there if you're not careful! (*Laughs.*) I swear, it's as if you've got to shave a battalion of eunuchs on punishment of death if you miss a single hair . . . and speaking of hair or . . . what was I saying? Oh yes. Beards. Speaking of that . . .

DOCTOR Troops should be discouraged from wearing facial hair. As the Romans first suggested . . .

CAPTAIN Yes, no beards. Quite right. (*To* WOYZECK.) And while we're on that subject—you haven't noticed any stray hair in your soup, have you now? Do you follow me? A hair from somebody else's beard perhaps? An engineer's or a sergeant's or even a . . . oh, say, a drum-major's? Well, Woyzeck? (*Beat.*) But that woman of yours . . . she's probably trustworthy, right? Isn't she?

WOYZECK Yes, sir. She's . . . what do you mean by all that, sir?

WOYZECK *moves close to the* CAPTAIN, *into his personal space. The* CAPTAIN *steps back, annoyed. The* DOCTOR *watches closely.*

CAPTAIN Look at his face! Look! (*Chortles.*) Well, perhaps not in your
food . . . but a hair caught in a pair of lips. Do you understand me
now? *Lips.* Ahh, love . . . believe me, I've known the feeling, too.
My God, Woyzeck . . . (*Studies him.*) You look white as death.

WOYZECK Captain, sir, please . . . I'm a poor man, I haven't got
much. Just her. Don't joke about this if you're not . . . please!

CAPTAIN Me, joke with you?! Why would I bother doing that?

The DOCTOR *moves to* WOYZECK, *placing a hand on his neck.*

DOCTOR Careful, Woyzeck, watch your pulse now! It's becoming
irregular and violent! Careful now!

WOYZECK The world's gone as hot as hell . . . but I feel like ice. Ice
cold. I'm all . . . (*Explodes.*) The bitch! SLUT! It *can't* be . . .

CAPTAIN Your eyes, my God . . . they're like a pair of knives! (*Steps
back.*) Stop it now or do you want me to put a bullet in your head?
I'm doing you a favor, Woyzeck, because you're not a bad sort . . .
I've told you for your own good.

DOCTOR Your face is growing taut, Woyzeck. It's twitching . . . your
muscles . . . and your behavior is tense. Excited.

WOYZECK I suppose anything is possible . . . (*Breaks.*) THE BITCH!!

WOYZECK *catches himself and stops, looking around; as if he had just
come upon the* DOCTOR *and the* CAPTAIN *now.*

WOYZECK It's a fine day, sir. Look. (*He points.*) A nice gray sky . . .
makes you want to pound a nail into it and hang yourself . . . all
because of the space between yes . . . and no. Tell me, Captain,
is the "no" to blame for the "yes," or the "yes" for the "no?" I'll . . .
I guess I'll need to think about that.

WOYZECK *executes a strange little bow and shuffles off—first slowly, then gathering speed. The* DOCTOR *follows after him.*

DOCTOR   What a case! Wait, Woyzeck!!

CAPTAIN   They make me so dizzy, all these people . . . (*Shudders.*)
Look at them go, that one tearing off like a spider's shadow and
the other jerking along behind him . . .

The sound of VOICES *rising up around the* CAPTAIN. *He spins around
and looks at the sky. Pulls up his collar.*

VOICES   WOYZECK . . . WOYZECK . . . WOYZECK!!

CAPTAIN   . . . like thunder following after lightning. It's grotesque,
I tell you. Grotesque!!

Blackout.

THE R∅∅M

MARIE *standing in one corner, fearfully watching* WOYZECK *as he hovers nearby. Staring at her. The baby asleep in a basket.*

WOYZECK . . . nothing. I can't see anything. Not at all. (*Squints.*) It should show on you! I should be able to spot it all over you . . . hold it in my hands.

MARIE What're you raving about, Franz? What's wrong?

WOYZECK Lots of people walk past, don't they? Down your street . . . and you can talk to anyone you choose. Can't you? (*Moves closer.*) Did he stand here . . . this close to you? Oh, I wish I'd been him!

MARIE What're you saying? I can't stop anyone from coming past. Walking by my window . . .

WOYZECK And your lips, so beautiful . . . they're not your fault, either, are they? (*Beat.*) A sin. Such a great, big, fat one like that . . . it stinks! Enough to knock the angels out of Heaven, and yet your lips . . . so red . . . and not a *mark* on them. (*Cries.*) Why? *Why* are you so beautiful, Marie? You're as lovely as sin itself.

MARIE You're delirious . . .

WOYZECK Did he stand right here? Just like this?!

MARIE Franz, the world is old . . . and it's been a long day. Many people can be in one place, one after the other after the next . . .

WOYZECK But I can see him! *Here*, with you.

MARIE You can see many things . . . as long as you're not blind and the sun is out.

WOYZECK . . . bitch!

This incenses WOYZECK, *who steps toward her suddenly and raises a fist. She steps back but holds her head up. Defiant.*

MARIE *Don't.* (*Firm.*) Don't you touch me. I'd rather have you put a knife in my guts than lay a hand on me. Not even my own father could do that If I looked at him, not since I was ten years old. And you won't either, not now.

WOYZECK Whore!

Slowly, though, WOYZECK *drops his hand and backs away. He stares at her. Studies her as he mumbles to himself.*

WOYZECK Still . . . it should show. Your sin. Even at the bottom of this abyss. (*Beat.*) She stands there, looking so innocent . . . but there's a stain on you. Yes. On your robe. (*Beat.*) Can I be sure? Who can ever be . . .?

WOYZECK *backs slowly away, his eyes growing wide. Exits.* MARIE *watches him go, then clutches her robe more tightly around herself as the baby starts to whimper. Stops.*

After a moment, MARIE *pulls a shawl around her shoulders and slips out through the front door.*

Sound of a beer hall band growing in intensity.

Blackout.

THE TAVERN

Filled with people and music. The band playing loudly in a corner. People dancing and drinking.

The DRUM-MAJOR, SERGEANT *and friends at one table.* ANDRES *alone at another. After a moment,* WOYZECK *enters. Glances around, then moves to* ANDRES *as he pours a drink. Downs it. Then another.*

WOYZECK . . . Andres!

ANDRES Huh?

WOYZECK Fine weather out, eh?

ANDRES Yes . . . *Sunday* weather. (*Points.*) Look, the band is playing. The girls're . . .

WOYZECK . . . dancing, Andres! They're all dancing!

ANDRES . . . sweating . . .

WOYZECK . . . at the Horse and Stars . . .

ANDRES . . . yes . . .

WOYZECK . . . they're dancing. Women, they love to dance! Dance, dance!!

ANDRES Suits me.

A few PATRONS *look over—most give* WOYZECK *no mind. The music plays on.*

After a moment, MARIE *wanders in but doesn't see* WOYZECK. *She moves toward the* DRUM-MAJOR *and they eye one another.*

WOYZECK *watches them;* ANDRES *watches him.*

WOYZECK Andres . . . look. (*Hands shaking.*) I can't sit still . . . I'm . . .

ANDRES   Don't be a fool, Franz.

WOYZECK   I've got to go over . . . see this for myself.

ANDRES   Don't be a troublemaker . . .

WOYZECK   I've *got* to!

ANDRES   . . . not because of that bitch.

WOYZECK   Ahhh! (*Pulls at his throat.*) It's so hot in here! Stifling!!

WOYZECK *moves toward the* DRUM-MAJOR *and* MARIE *but takes his time, circling them. He moves through a boisterous crowd, catching snatches of conversation and laughter.*

PATRON 1   . . . I've got a shirt on, yes, but it's not my own!

PATRON 2   . . . let me punch a hole through your face, brother! As any friend would do!

PATRON 3   . . . my soul is filthy! It stinks like home-made wine!

PATRON 4   . . . I wish our noses were the necks of bottles. We could pour 'em down each other's throats!

PATRON 5   . . . I'm so sad I could weep buckets tonight!

PATRON 6   . . . I'm twice the man he is! Twice!

WOYZECK *comes to a stop in the shadows—the* DRUM-MAJOR *has his hands all over* MARIE, *who is laughing.* WOYZECK *holds his head in agony.*

All the PATRONS, *from their previous positions, turn to him and call out:*

PATRONS   WOYZECK . . . WOYZECK . . . WOYZECK!!

WOYZECK *turns to look but they have already returned to their conversations, friends, etc.* WOYZECK *looks back at* MARIE *and the* DRUM-MAJOR, *who begin to dance now.*

WOYZECK   Her. And him. Hell. *Hell*! Oh, damnation!!

DRUM-MAJOR   Here we go . . . round and round . . .

WOYZECK . . . round and round . . .

MARIE . . . on and on . . .

WOYZECK . . . on and on and on and ON!! On it goes, the music and
dancing, round and round and on!!!

WOYZECK *lurches off in the opposite direction as* MARIE *and the* DRUM-
MAJOR *stop, panting and laughing. They move off toward the door,
hands all over the other.*

WOYZECK *watches them go—he explodes when they are gone.
Screaming loudly enough for the band to stop. People gawk and
stare.*

WOYZECK God in Heaven, why can't you blow out the sun?! Let
them fall onto each other in darkness . . . but hide their sins from
me!! Filth and flesh and male, female, man and beast!! They do
it in the open, like flies on the back of my hand!!! (*Beat.*) She's
like a bitch in heat! SLUT!!

ANDRES *comes to his friend and tries to help but* WOYZECK *shakes him
off. Moves away and slips. Falls to the floor.*

WOYZECK He's . . . he's got his hands all over her. *Pawing* her . . .
like I did once. In the beginning . . .

WOYZECK *slumps down as he passes out.* ANDRES *reaches down,
slaps his face. Nothing. He moves to the bar for water while one of
the* PATRONS *wanders over and stands behind him.*

PATRON 1 Brethren! (*Indicating.*) Think now about the Wanderer,
who does stand beside the stream of time as he communes
with himself, wondering, "Wherefore is man?" (*Grins.*) Verily
I say unto you, how could any of us—the cooper, the cobbler,

the doctor—how could we live if God had not created Man? Or how might the tailor work his trade if God had not placed "shame" into the human beast? Likewise, where would this soldier be if he hadn't been fitted with the desire for self-destruction?

Cheers from the crowd; the PATRON *bows but holds up a hand for silence.*

PATRON 1 Yes, yes, that's all very well . . . but earthly things are evil. Money worst of all. So, in summation . . . (*Laughs.*) . . . let's piss on a cross and go kill ourselves a Jew!!

The PATRON *raises his glass, then pours it onto* WOYZECK, *who starts to come to. Laughter and more cheering.*

ANDRES *comes back and helps* WOYZECK *to his feet. Together they move back to a table.* ANDRES *helps* WOYZECK *drink.*

WOYZECK . . . Andres . . . Andres . . .

ANDRES What's the matter?

WOYZECK Everything is spinning . . . when my eyes are shut . . . I hear the music and on it goes, round and round and on . . . (*Eyes widening.*) Voices, too. I hear them! Andres, can't you hear that?!

ANDRES No, Franz . . . (*Looks around.*) It's only the dancers, let them be . . . I'm tired.

WOYZECK It keeps saying, "Stab! Stab!" All the time, between my eyes like a knife. "Stab! STAB!!"

ANDRES . . . God save us . . .

The DRUM-MAJOR *returns and gathers up his helmet that he left behind. He goes to the* SERGEANT. *Whispers in his ear and they both laugh. Loudly.* WOYZECK *turns and sees him.* ANDRES *grabs for him but is too late;* WOYZECK *runs across the room and plows into the man. The* DRUM-MAJOR *stumbles but* WOYZECK *hits the floor. Jumps back up.*

DRUM-MAJOR You looking for a fight? Huh?! I'm a man! You hear me, a man!! (*Waves* WOYZECK *away.*) Go have a drink . . . I wish the world was made of booze! Drink up, soldier!!

The DRUM-MAJOR *turns away and* WOYZECK *pushes him again.*

DRUM-MAJOR You little shit!!! I'll pull out your tongue and wrap it around your throat! I'll rip the breath right out of you . . . you'll fart like an old woman when I'm through!!

WOYZECK *says nothing—just whistles. The* DRUM-MAJOR *is angered and attacks. A fight ensues.* ANDRES *goes to help but is subdued by the* SERGEANT. *The crowd roars.*

WOYZECK *is soundly beaten and left in a heap. The* DRUM-MAJOR *stands and walks off. Winded. As he goes:*

DRUM-MAJOR Now the prick can whistle 'til he is blue in the face!

The DRUM-MAJOR *exits with a tip of his helmet to the* SERGEANT. ANDRES *breaks free and goes to help* WOYZECK.

SERGEANT . . . he's had it.

PATRON 3 . . . spent . . .

PATRON 2 . . . a bellyful . . .

PATRON 4 . . . he's bleeding . . .

WOYZECK *sits on a bench, leaning on* ANDRES. *Beaten.*

WOYZECK . . . one thing after the next.

Laughter rises from where the SERGEANT *is standing—he is talking to a small group of men.*

WOYZECK What's he saying?

ANDRES Nothing. Just talking to a friend, is all . . .

WOYZECK He said something! What's that he said?

ANDRES Franz, what's it matter?

SERGEANT . . . and he tells me . . . (*Laughs.*) "A fine little piece . . . fantastic hot thighs . . . like sizzling butter!"

More laughter as the music starts again. WOYZECK *sits and stares off.* ANDRES *tries to maintain the peace.*

WOYZECK . . . so that's what he said. (*Beat.*) What was it I said before? About a knife? Such silly things . . . our dreams . . .

WOYZECK *gets to his feet, heads toward the door.* ANDRES *stands, watching him go.*

ANDRES Where are you off to?

WOYZECK For wine . . . my Captain's wine for tomorrow. Must have some. (*Beat.*) I'll tell you, though, Andres . . . there wasn't another one like her.

ANDRES Who, Franz?

WOYZECK Doesn't matter. See you . . .

WOYZECK *stops at the bar, buys a bottle of red wine.*

A wave of the hand as he pushes his way out of the place. ANDRES *sits back down. Drinks.*

Blackout.

THE WOODS

Sounds of the night. WOYZECK *wandering along, listening to the animals and staring up at the moon. Noises build and he holds his hands to his ears.*

WOYZECK   . . . on and on, round and round! On and on and on!! The sounds around me, they just won't stop!!!

VOICES   WOYZECK . . . WOYZECK . . . WOYZECK!!

WOYZECK   There! Who's that, speaking to me?

He throws himself down onto the ground, listening.

WOYZECK   What're you saying to me?! What?!! Just SAY it!! Louder . . . LOUDER . . .

VOICES   WOYZECK . . . WOYZECK . . . WOYZECK!!

WOYZECK   ". . . stab . . . stab the she-wolf. Stab her dead?" (*Beat.*) Must I? *Must* I?!

WOYZECK *stands, looking up at the trees, the moon.*

WOYZECK   Is it even there in the wind?! Do I hear it there, too?!!

He staggers around in circles, listening. Moaning.

VOICES   WOYZECK . . . WOYZECK . . . WOYZECK!!

WOYZECK   "Stab her . . . stab her . . . stab HER!"

WOYZECK *throws the bottle, shattering it. Silence.*

WOYZECK   . . . dead.

Blackout.

THE PAWNSHOP

A shack owned by a Jew—an establishment on the edge of town.

The JEW *is inside, counting something.* KARL *is nearby and holding things up to inspect them by candlelight.* WOYZECK *enters and nods to the* JEW, *looks around. Brushes past* KARL *and approaches the counter.*

JEW . . . what's this one want? (*To* WOYZECK.) Well?

WOYZECK Guns?

JEW Perhaps.

WOYZECK Yes or no?

JEW Per-haps . . .

WOYZECK How much?

JEW Depends. How much you have?

WOYZECK *shrugs. The* JEW *holds up five fingers. Then four.* WOYZECK *shrugs again; the* JEW *mimics him.*

WOYZECK That's a lot.

JEW You buy or you don't. It's late.

WOYZECK *waves him off, continues to look around.* KARL *gets too close and* WOYZECK *shoos him away. Finally* WOYZECK *points at another counter.*

WOYZECK . . . and the knife. How much?

JEW That one? (*Smiles.*) Lovely and so straight it is . . . you want to cut your throat with it? No matter. I give it to you cheap, same price as anybody else. Death can come easy . . . but not for *nothing*. Everything costs money. Even death.

WOYZECK Huh. (*Touches it.*) I bet I could cut more than *bread* with
   that . . .

JEW Yes.

WOYZECK *picks it up and tries it—slicing it through the air a few times.
The* JEW *smiles at* WOYZECK *and holds up two fingers.* WOYZECK *nods
and reaches into a pocket; tosses two coins onto the table.*

WOYZECK Here. Take it.

Without waiting, WOYZECK *tucks the knife away and heads for the door.
Exits.*

The JEW *watches him go, then spits. Collects up the coins and hides
them away.*

JEW "Here!" like it was nothing. "Take it," he says! Like I was a dog
   . . . (*Beat.*) Well, it's all money. All the same to me . . .

Blackout.

THE BARRACKS

ANDRES *asleep on his bunk*—WOYZECK *standing over him, his knife in one hand. Silence.*

After a moment, WOYZECK *puts the knife away and lies down on his own cot. Tossing and turning. Finally he gets up and shakes* ANDRES *awake.* ANDRES *sits up, groggy.*

ANDRES . . . it's late.

WOYZECK *Early.*

ANDRES Well, whatever it is, it's that.

WOYZECK Yes.

WOYZECK *pulls a battered box out from beneath his bed. Opens it. Holds up a vest.*

WOYZECK A waistcoat. Not standard issue, but you might find some use for it . . .

ANDRES Yes.

WOYZECK Here . . . (*Produces jewelry.*) This cross was my sister's. (*Kisses it.*) And this ring. Take them.

WOYZECK *hands them over and keeps rummaging.* ANDRES *turns the items over in the darkness.*

ANDRES Fine. (*Beat.*) Franz . . . ?

WOYZECK *holds up a finger to quiet him. Produces a small picture.*

WOYZECK Shhhh . . . we don't want to wake the others. (*Beat.*) I've got this, too. A holy picture, with two hearts on it. And real gold.

See the legend? "Oh Lord, as your wounds were red with blood, so let mine own be." (*Smiles.*) My mother won't miss it. She's got no feeling left in her hands to hold it with . . . only when the sun shines on them.

ANDRES Alright.

WOYZECK Ahh. (*Reads from paper.*) "Friedrich Johann Franz Woyzeck. A rifleman. Fourth company, Second Battalion. Second Regiment. Born on the feast of the Annunciation." I am thirty years old. Seven months and twelve days.

ANDRES . . . you read well, Franz.

WOYZECK Yes . . . and write, too. But they do not want to know that! See?

WOYZECK *looks around, then pulls his little notebook out of one pocket. Puts on his glasses. Leans in and whispers a passage to* ANDRES.

WOYZECK " . . . the relationship between rich and poor is . . . the only revolutionary element in the world. Hunger alone can become the . . . goddess of freedom. Give us one square meal and the revolution would soon die of apoplexy . . . "

ANDRES . . . dangerous thoughts, Franz.

WOYZECK Yes. (*Hands over the bundle.*) Read it some time. When you're ready.

ANDRES *Subversive* thoughts! It's . . . (*He feels* WOYZECK*'s head.*) You should report sick, Franz. You need some schnapps with a powder in it. That might break your fever . . .

WOYZECK Yes. You never know . . .

ANDRES What? Know what?

WOYZECK . . . about the carpenter . . .

ANDRES I don't understand. You're not at all well, Franz . . .

WOYZECK . . . when he collects his shavings to put in the coffin. You
never know whose head will lie on them. Maybe even his *own* . . .

WOYZECK *smiles sadly at his friend—then disappears into the darkness.*
Exits.

ANDRES *sits back down on his bed with the loot. Looks around, then*
slowly opens the notebook. Begins to read.

Blackout.

THE WØØDS

WOYZECK *leading* MARIE *through the woods—holding back the branches for her, placing a hand on her shoulders, etc. Sounds of the night all around. Moon still out.*

MARIE . . . it's so dark, Franz.

WOYZECK Mmmmm.

MARIE There . . . (*Yawns.*) . . . that must be the town over that way.

WOYZECK Yes. Let's rest a moment . . .

MARIE No, I have to get back. The baby.

WOYZECK He's fine. Asleep.

MARIE You don't come by all yesterday. Not at all . . . now this! What're we doing out *here*?

WOYZECK Come and sit down.

MARIE I have to go.

WOYZECK No, you'll get sore feet . . . I want to save you from that.

MARIE What's the matter with you? Why're you going on like this?!

WOYZECK *sits on his haunches near the edge of a pond.*

WOYZECK How long's it's been? Do you know?

MARIE For us? Two years on Easter.

WOYZECK Two years . . . (*To himself.*) And just imagine how long it's going to be . . .

MARIE This is idiotic! I've got to go home now, Franz. The baby's . . .

The sentence trails off as she stops, pulling her shawl around her shoulders. Shivering. WOYZECK *gets up and helps her.*

WOYZECK Are you cold, Marie? (*Pulls her close.*) But you're warm
to touch. Your lips, still hot . . . breath is like fire. A *harlot's* mouth.

MARIE *pulls away and stands her ground, defiant.* WOYZECK *circles her.*

MARIE . . . Franz . . .

WOYZECK I'd give anything to kiss you a last time . . . (*Beat.*)
Feel cold, do you? *Deathly* cold . . . but you won't feel the dew
come morning.

MARIE What're you saying?

WOYZECK Nothing. Not anything . . .

MARIE *steps back again, looking around. Up.*

MARIE The moon is out. Look how red it is . . .

WOYZECK Yes. Like blood dripping off a blade . . .

MARIE What does that mean? (*Studies him.*) Franz, what's . . .
you're *so* pale.

*Only now does she see the knife appear in his hands—and before
she can scream* WOYZECK *has her around the neck. Holds a finger to
his lips. She nods. He forces her to her knees.*

WOYZECK . . . pray, Marie. Pray now.

MARIE Franz . . . (*He pushes her.*) Oh God, I beg thee to . . . "And
the scribes and the pharisees brought him a woman taken in adul-
tery . . . and Jesus said unto her: 'Neither do I condemn thee. Go
now, and sin no more . . .'" (*Starts to cry.*) Give me strength to
pray! Dear God, I cannot . . .

She glances up to see WOYZECK *raising the knife over his head.* MARIE
*screams and tries to get to her feet. She trips over her skirts and rolls
to one side.* WOYZECK *sits on her as he brings the knife down.*

MARIE Stop, Franz, no! God, help me!!

WOYZECK Take that! That!! There, there!!!

MARIE HELP!!

WOYZECK Why can't you die?! There! There!! On and on and ON!!!
(*Stabbing her.*) Still moving? (*Stabs.*) Still?! And still?!!!

WOYZECK *stops; his sleeves are covered in blood.* MARIE *is face-down, silent.*

WOYZECK . . . now are you dead? Dead? *Dead?*

The VOICES *start in again. Low at first, but rising.*

VOICES WOYZECK . . . WOYZECK . . . WOYZECK!

WOYZECK *drops the knife to cover his ears—he runs off and away. Into the shadows.*

MARIE *lies where she fell. No movement. Sounds of the night around her.*

Blackout.

THE TAVERN

The same as before, but most of the PATRONS *are long gone now. A barmaid clearing up. A few people at tables, still drinking.* MARGARET *with* PATRON 5, *dancing.* KARL *drunk (with his crutches nearby).*

After a moment, WOYZECK *enters and crosses to the bar. His eyes are wild. Moves toward the dancing couple.*

WOYZECK . . . go on, dance! Dance, dance, we all should dance!! Before he comes to get us . . .

WOYZECK *goes to the bar, downs a drink.*

WOYZECK I'm hot, so hot . . . (*Feeling his head.*) That's the way the devil works—takes one and lets the others go.

WOYZECK *watches the dancers and suddenly jumps up. Pushes* MARGARET'S *partner away and grabs her up in his arms.*

WOYZECK Sit down, you! (*To* MARGARET.) Hot, you are. Burning up. Why's that? (*Grabs her face.*) But you want to be careful, Margaret, or you'll end up cold . . . cold, I say!

MARGARET *pulls his hand away from her face—is about to drop it but holds on, staring at his fingertips.*

WOYZECK Sorry, yes . . . i wouldn't want to make a mess of you.
MARGARET What's this? Here? (*Touching his hand.*) On your fingertips?
WOYZECK On me? Where?

PATRON 5 They're covered in red . . .

MARGARET . . . blood. (*Looks at her fingers.*) It's *blood.*

WOYZECK Blood? *Blood*?!

The music comes to a halt. Silence. The others begin to gather around. WOYZECK *backs up.*

PATRON 1 Ewwww . . . blood.

WOYZECK I must've . . . I've cut myself.

MARGARET Where?

WOYZECK On the hand. I cut my hand or something . . .

PATRON 5 Then how'd it get on your elbow? There . . . (*Points.*) How?

WOYZECK When I wiped it. Off.

MARGARET Then you're a genuis . . .

WOYZECK What do you mean?

MARGARET That hand on the same elbow. (*She mimes it.*) No . . .

KARL, *still drunk in a corner, uses his crutches to stand and calls out:*

KARL Fee-fie-fo-fum, I smell the blood of a dead some-one!

WOYZECK *looks over at him—*KARL *pretends to stab at him with an imaginary knife. Laughs. The others watch, then turn back to* WOYZECK.

WOYZECK What the hell are you looking at? Huh? What's it to any of you?!

*The circle tightens—*WOYZECK *moves backward toward the door.*

WOYZECK WHAT'RE YOU ALL LOOKING AT?!!

The VOICES *begin in again. Louder and louder.* WOYZECK *has to cover his ears.*

VOICES WOYZECK . . . WOYZECK . . . WOYZECK!!

WOYZECK STOP IT!! STOP!!! (*Beat.*) What do you think I am . . .
a murderer? Hmm? Look at *yourselves* . . .

One of the PATRONS *steps forward, puts a hand on* WOYZECK'S *shoulder.*
WOYZECK *begins to shake violently and pushes the man away.*

WOYZECK Out of my way! Get away!!

WOYZECK *turns and runs out. Exits. The others turn and look at each
other, mumbling.* KARL *laughs and bangs his hands on the table.*

KARL . . . once upon a time there was a little boy.

Blackout.

THE WØØDS

MARIE *where she fell. Silent.* WOYZECK *appears after a moment, searching through the branches and high grass.*

WOYZECK . . . what is this place? (*Searching.*) What's that noise?!

WOYZECK *continues to move through the woods. Wandering.*

WOYZECK . . . where is it? Is it here? Where? I'm getting closer. Closer. I left It here . . . where's the knife?!

WOYZECK *stumbles across* MARIE *and lets out a gasp. He looks around, then kneels near her. Scoops her up into his arms.*

WOYZECK Marie. (*Holds her tight.*) So still. So, so . . . nothing. Not a sound. Why are you so pale, Marie? (*Kissing her.*) Marie . . . oh my Marie! (*Cries.*) What's that red around your neck, love? Is it a necklace? Is it to go along with your earrings? Did he give it to you for that . . . for your sins. So black what you did. Black, black sins, Marie. Did I whiten you again . . .? (*Touches her hair.*) Your hair is so tangled . . . Didn't you braid it today?

WOYZECK *kisses her. Long and soft. Then sounds in the distance— an owl perhaps—spook him.* WOYZECK *looks up.*

WOYZECK The knife! I've got to . . .

WOYZECK *searches around, finds it. He thinks for a bit, then tosses it into the water. A soft plop!*

WOYZECK In you go . . . (*Watches.*) Sink like a dark stone in the water. (*Waits.*) No . . . it's too close. Much too . . . they swim here. It's not right.

WOYZECK *wades into the water up to his boots. Looks.*

WOYZECK And in the summer, when the young boys dive deep, deep to the bottom of the pond . . . what then? It'll . . . it'd be rusty by then. Yes? If I'd broken it, the blade . . . then no one could recognize it. Not even that Jew.

WOYZECK *moves a bit deeper into the water. Dips his hands in—he glances at them as they come out. Dripping.*

WOYZECK Is there still blood on me? I need to wash it off! Wash myself . . . ahh, there's a spot . . . and another one. There. And there. And there, too. And still one more . . .

WOYZECK *slowly disappears beneath the surface. All traces of him are gone. Silence.*

Blackout.

THE POND

WOYZECK *in a wave of blue—drifting slowly to the bottom of the pond. Spinning and dropping through the water.*

(*We can also see* ANDRES *on his bunk, reading slowly aloud from* WOYZECK*'s notebook. Flipping to various passages.*)

ANDRES ". . . we must act according to our principles . . . the essential needs of the masses can bring about a change . . . all this activity— the shouts of the individual—is a foolish waste of time . . . no one hears them . . . no one helps them, either . . . the poor patiently pull the cart while the princes and the liberals play out their farces . . . my first moment of clarity for a week . . . constant headaches and a fever . . . swallowed by a sea of my thoughts which dissolve all my senses . . . every face seems to me a death's head, the eyes glazed, the cheeks like wax . . . what is it in us that lies and murders and steals?. . . darkness hovers over me, my heart grown wide with endless longing . . . I am no longer able to even indulge myself in pain . . . I am an automaton . . . my soul has been taken away . . . our age is now totally materialistic but what we need is weapons and bread . . . they try to tell us 'all republics are impossible,' so every day good Germans are told about anarchy, murder and manslaughter . . . yet . . . if anything can help in our time, then it is violence. Indeed, are we not . . . already in a constant state of violence?"

WOYZECK'S *lifeless body comes to rest on the bottom of the pond. Bobbing in the lazy current.*

ANDRES *looks up, nervous, and quickly hides the notebook under his pillow.*

The water and WOYZECK *are gone now—disappearing into the darkness.* ANDRES *huddles alone in his bunk. Eyes open.*

Blackout.

THE ØPERATING THEATER

Two bodies on gurneys stand before us. Their hands fall out from beneath the sheets—almost as if they were being held in death.

Two attendants pull back the covers as the DOCTOR *enters the room. He goes to a table full of tools and starts in immediately on* WOYZECK*— measuring, poking, prodding.*

DOCTOR . . . oh, *Woyzeck.* (*Shakes his head.*) Age: 30 years; height: 6 shoes, 9 inches of the new Hessian measurement; Hair: fair; Forehead: very prominent; Eyebrows: fair; Eyes: gray; Nose: strong; Mouth: small; Beard: fair; Chin: round; Stature: strong, slim; Complexion: fresh. (*Laughs.*) Well, it *used* to be . . .

The others politely laugh. The DOCTOR *chortles again.*

DOCTOR Let's see now, what did we leave out?

ATTENDANT 1 Ummm . . . face?

DOCTOR Hmmm. Funny, I couldn't tell you without looking. (*Grins.*) Take a peek . . . (*Studies* WOYZECK.) Oval. Anything else?

ATTENDANT 1 No. Well, any other particular characteristics . . . ?

DOCTOR . . . yes. The man was short-sighted.

ATTENDANT 1 And name? His first name, please?

DOCTOR . . . hmm. I can't honestly recall.

The DOCTOR *goes about the body, checking this and that—an* ATTENDANT *taking notes as he goes.*

DOCTOR . . . Still, it's a good murder he's done. A really lovely murder . . . Couldn't wish for a nicer job . . . we haven't had one of this caliber in years! (*Beat.*) So that's something.

The DOCTOR *stops his check-up and moves to another set of tools— selects a bone saw and turns to* WOYZECK'S *head. He starts in on the skull, cutting into the flesh. The sound of metal on bone. Blood spilling onto the tiled flooring. Sickening.*

Only now do we see KARL *sitting in a corner—seated on an upturned bedpan. Watching. Lights are slowly fading. He lights a match, holding it close to his face.*

KARL   . . . once upon a time there was a poor little boy who had no mother or father. Everyone was dead and there was no one left in the whole world. Everything was quite . . .

He blows it out. The stage is flooded in blackness.

KARL   . . . *dead.*

The sound of the saw continues—cutting and cutting and cutting. On and on and on.

The sound of a beer hall band begins to build. Growing in intensity.

Blackout.

THE BARRACKS

ANDRES *picks up a bowl and razor. He begins to shave the* CAPTAIN, *who is seated.*

CAPTAIN   . . . careful, Andres. Be careful. One step after the next. (*Beat.*) You make me nervous. What should I do with the few moments you save rushing this way? What good will they do me?

ANDRES *steadies his hand and forcibly slows down.*

CAPTAIN   Think, Andres. Really think about this. You've got, what, another thirty years left? Thirty good years. *Thirty.* (*Beat.*) You've got to space it out, man! (*Beat.*) What else can you do with such an *enormous* amount of time?

ANDRES   Yes, sir.

CAPTAIN   I worry about the world, Andres, the idea of eternity. What is it? Eternity is eternity is eternity. Anyone can see that. But it's also not that, not just that. Eternity. It's just one beat as well . . . yes . . . just one single beat. It's rather horrifying, how life turns about in a day. What a waste! And what does it all *mean*, anyway? I can't bear to look at the miller's wheel any more, when I pass it. I look away. It's too depressing.

ANDRES   Yes, sir.

The CAPTAIN *is frustrated and shrugs off* ANDRES *for a moment, studying him.* ANDRES *waits.*

CAPTAIN You men always seem so frightened! Good people don't look like that, Andres. Not a person with a clean conscience.

ANDRES *nods, then returns to his shaving. The* CAPTAIN *eyes him suspiciously, then closes his eyes.*

ANDRES Yes, sir.

CAPTAIN That's right . . . that's it . . . slowly. Slowly now . . .

The sound of VOICES *now, growing in intensity.*

VOICES ANDRES . . . ANDRES . . . ANDRES!

ANDRES *looks around, shakes his head. Tries to get back to his work.*

VOICES ANDRES . . . ANDRES . . . ANDRES!!

CAPTAIN Slowly, man, that's the way. Do it slowly . . . you have all the time in the world . . .

ANDRES *slowly raises the razor over his head. His eyes widening as his mouth opens into a scream. The sound of a beer hall band grows louder and louder. Nearly unbearable.*

Silence. Darkness.

KANDAHAR

Silence. Darkness.

A MAN *sitting in a chair. Staring straight ahead. A harsh light on his face. He doesn't seem to mind.*

He sits in silence for a moment. Or two. Drumming fingers on the table to a beat in his head.

Finally:

MAN   . . . she made me do it. (*Beat.*) And I know you hear people say that, all the time, but it's true. She made me. Somehow she did. I know she did. She made all of it happen. All this. (*Beat.*) Women have that power . . . you know what I mean? They do . . . it's, like, a *secret* power inside of 'em. They really do have it, I'm not just saying that or, you know . . . using it as an excuse . . . I've always felt that and it's true. They have this *thing* inside them, this way of being and thinking and acting . . . and they use it on us to get us to do stuff without us guys even realizing it. It's true. That's a real phenomenon. Their mysterious ways. My dad, he told me about it and I believe he was accurate . . . to some degree, at least. (*Beat.*) Anyway, if that's true or it's not—in a general sense, I mean—I still believe that she made me do all the stuff that's happened here. I'm saying in a more specific way. What I've done . . . how I went off and, you know . . . all the damage I did . . . that was *her* doing . . . she brought that down upon herself. And me. And everybody else.

He waits. Thinking. Watching. Motionless in his chair.

She planted those seeds in my head—what set me off, made me go ballistic, is what I'm saying—long before I ever went over for my last tour. Over there to Kandahar. (*Beat.*) Even before I left I was thinking those things. Thinking about doing that stuff. To her. To her or to some people. Other people that we knew in our lives. I swear I was. (*Beat.*) She has a way of getting inside my head . . . getting in there and forcing me to do things for her . . . and to her . . . things that I never couldn't even dreamed about when I was a kid. No way. Uh-uh. Some of that shit was stuff I never could've come up with on my own . . . or as a child. No. It took a woman like her to make me have any of those type thoughts. (*Beat.*) Seriously.

He wipes at his eyes. Blinking. Trying to concentrate on what he's saying.

And I was a good kid, too. Everybody said that . . . when I was younger? Everybody did. I was, like, a nice boy. Not a gold star type child, not like that, or some fancy straight A student—in fact, my dad even had one of those things, those stickers for your car, a bumper sticker, that he found at a truck stop somewhere, and it said—this was on an old Monte Carlo he would drive around—he had this sticker and it read: "MY KID BEATS UP HONOR ROLL STUDENTS AT JEFFERSON JUNIOR HIGH." That made him laugh, that fucking sticker did. He would see that, no matter when, and he would bust out laughing and he had a big laugh, this guy. My dad. This high sorta laugh that came outta him and could take over a room or on the street or wherever. He loved that thing. But it wasn't true; about me hurting other kids or that type of deal. I was nice back then. A really nice guy in those days . . . in high school, too. For that matter. Really good to all the others around me—and I was

in class with some real dicks, too, so . . . but yeah, I was very re-
spectful and all that shit. I mean, pretty much. Everybody has their
days but overall, that's what I'm saying is *overall* . . . I was a good
person. That's from my mom, that side of me . . . I should be clear
about that, she was the person who brought out the sunnier side of
me at that age, not my dad. He didn't do shit for me. Ever. Except
laugh at that fucking bumper sticker of his . . . (*Beat.*) But see? I'm
not blaming all women for what's happened to me, or saying that
they're all crazy or psycho or whatnot, I'm not. I like women. My
mom was a real great lady and I loved her. Right up to the moment
she passed . . . and I mean there on her hospital bed . . . I was
blown away by her. As a person. Yeah. She was great. (*Beat.*)
Women are just fine . . . but they do have those powers I was talking about earlier. They really do.

He nods at this, drifting off as he thinks about her or something else.
Silent for a beat.

But that's not why I'm here . . . right? Why you got me sitting here
and talking. You want some answers to what happened, don't
you? Over there at the base yesterday . . . that's what we're doing
here, am I right? Sure. I get it. I *understand*. And that's cool by me.
It is. (*Beat.*) I already told you about my wife . . . what she was
able to do to me . . . how she can make me feel with just one
word, or, like, not even that . . . without a single word spoken. No.
Just a look. She can look at me and make me so fucking hot for
her or, you know, angry or happy . . . that's what she can do.
Since the day I met her. Yeah. (*Beat.*) And she likes it . . . *enjoys* it
. . . that power over me. She does. Turns it off and on like some
light switch or not even that, the kind that doesn't even need a
switch . . . you just clap your hands and the lights go off and on.

(*Claps his hands.*) BAM!! (*Claps again.*) Like that. (*Claps again.*)
BAM!! Off and on. Off and on. That's what she'd do to me . . .
just by looking me in the eye. Just like that product you've seen
on the TV . . . (*Claps his hands.*) BAM!

*He stops and fidgets for a moment. Take a sip of water from a glass in
front of him. Smiles.*

You probably don't believe that. Don't wanna believe that she
could do a thing like that to me . . . or care that she's got that
ability. That doesn't answer all of your questions . . . doesn't
close the book on your investigations . . . right? No. That doesn't
do the trick, I'm sure. You need the HOWS and WHYS and all
that shit from me before we're through and that's okay. I get it.
I knew we'd end up over here, somehow I already knew that . . .
that we'd have to do this part at some point. Based on what I did.
And all that. Because I was never gonna kill myself, do myself in
at any point, no way. Uh-uh. That was *not* part of the deal. Not
ever. Like some fucking pussy who goes into a *mall* or whatever,
starts tearing the place up and then sticks a shotgun in his mouth
at the end of it. Or some little high school guy, dressed in camo
and goes off on a shooting spree in his home room but kills himself
before the cops get there and can make a fair fight of it? Nope.
I'm not one of those types so . . . yeah . . . I figured I was gonna
end up in a place like this along the way. At some point. (*Beat.*)
Lemme ask you something . . . you've seen combat, right, all of
you? (*Waits.*) Yeah? (*Waits.*) Okay then. (*Beat.*) You ever kill anybody? Any of you? (*Beat.*) I guess you wouldn't tell me if you had
. . . or don't want to, maybe, but I bet at least a few of you have
. . . probably more. Overseas or over there on the base. Some
guy like me, did shit to people . . . no doubt you've had to bring

him down. Take 'em out. No doubt about it. Of *course* you have.
Come on . . . you can tell me. (*Beat.*) I'm just asking . . .

He waits another beat. Nothing in return. He shrugs as he sits there.

Whatever. Doesn't matter. Can't change at all what I've done, but
I just thought we might talk about it, compare stories and that
sorta thing, but it's no big deal . . . doesn't alter the facts. Right?
Nope. Not one little bit. (*Beat.*) There was this guy I got deployed
with, that last time. And she started in with him. Messing around.
You know what I'm saying . . . right? You've checked all that out
already. That side of the story. About him. And her. What they've
done. Sure you have. (*Beat.*) I'm not saying she *picked* him, like,
chose him over some of the other guys because she knew we'd
end up together over there but you have to wonder . . . don't
you? You have to know that's gonna run in and out of your brain
a thousand times, whether she's really that cold or not. Capable
of such calibrated shit or not . . . wait, that's not the right word . . .
not that . . . I mean "calculated." Don't I? Yeah, I think so. If she
could be that mean . . . and calculated . . . and all that . . . (*Beat.*)
And *Yes* is the answer, if you're asking. She could do that and
then some. That's just her nature. To be that way. To hurt me.
(*Beat.*) But I got her back, though . . . didn't I? Got her back and
then some . . . (*Beat.*) Yep. I sure did.

*He smiles a little, to himself. As if he's savoring a private joke. And
then it passes. He begins in again:*

Over there in Afghanistan, it's like . . . you know . . . the Wild West
or some shit. I mean that. Not that they don't have a lotta, like,
restaurants and, you know, snack foods and places for Wi-Fi
and all that stuff, because they do. They totally do, but it's just

. . . different. Walking on a street and you never know what's gonna happen next. A car blows up . . . some kid is gonna try to give you broken glass in a soda pop . . . it's just day-by-day when you serve in a place like that. Not sure who cares or wants to kill you. That's just how it is. (*Beat.*) And a guy can get himself shot over there, real easy. Or whatever. Captain was always saying that to us, and this doctor that I was seeing . . . not just me but a lot of guys, 'cause of the stress and, you know . . . just because. They were always telling us to be alert but to try and relax. Yeah, that's a good idea! I mean, what the fuck? How are you gonna do those two things at once? Huh? I dunno. Doesn't matter. (*Beat.*) I found an email from her—my wife—to this guy one time, he got up from one of the base computers there, stood up from his seat and walked away . . . I wandered over to use it next, I swear I wasn't following him or trying to see what he was up to, but the guy forgot to log out and so all his shit is . . . you know . . . it's right there . . . so I flicked through his things and there it was. From her. HOTLIPS69. (*Beat.*) The first part came from that one show about the hospital. *M*A*S*H*. That's where she got that. The "69" is probably sort of self-explanatory . . . she thought it was funny. (*Beat.*) I read the thing a couple times. Printed it off. Carried it around in my wallet. (*Looking out.*) You've got my stuff, right? It's in there if you wanna read it. (*Beat.*) Doesn't say too much. Weather back home. A couple bits about working at the Commissary, which she did for awhile, and then a few lines about him. And her. And his cock. And a little part about his upcoming birthday. (*Beat.*) Anyway, the whole thing's just so fucking pathetic . . . right? So usual and normal. Shit happens all the time, and people go on with their lives . . . and so the captain keeps telling me to take it easy and the doctor is always asking questions as he gives me another bottle to fill up with my piss . . . after a month or two, it starts to wear you down. (*Beat.*) Anyhow, that's not what you asked. The answer to what you asked is: I probably shot about seven or eight guys while I was in Kandahar . . . maybe ten . . . and almost every one of 'em was in an actual firefight . . . but I gotta admit, since we're here now and this is the time for it, I guess . . . I was practicing on a couple of 'em. I was. I'm not ashamed to say that, or . . . angry or sad, even . . . I guess I don't feel very much about it at all. It's just the truth so I thought I should tell you . . . that's what happened and that's what I did. (*Beat.*) I did that. I practiced on 'em a little bit over there . . .

He stares out at the light. Squinting. Takes a drink and then continues.

When we got back to the States—me and my company, I'm saying—I spent a nice couple days with my wife. She was sweet and seemed happy to see me. In her way. But I knew what was up . . . how she really felt . . . about me. And us. And all that. (*Beat.*) I fucked her that first night I was home but it was dark in the room so I couldn't really see her face and she couldn't see mine . . . I think she liked it, but who knows? How can you ever really tell with somebody? Ask 'em, I guess . . . or listen to 'em, during it, I mean . . . but who knows what's really in their hearts? Down there in their *heart* of hearts? (*Beat.*) Not me. Don't ask me . . .

The MAN *stretches a bit. Stops. Looking around. Finally he starts in again.*

Anyway, yeah . . . one morning I got up and made breakfast—I've always been a pretty early riser—and I ate and cleaned it up and all that, and then I took that email outta my wallet and put it there on her pillow, next to her. So she'd see it as she woke up. (*Beat.*) She slept late, the way she always did . . . but I was there on the bed. Waiting. When she finally woke . . . eyes fluttering open really slowly, the first thing she saw was that paper. The words she'd written, right there next to her face. Her eyes focused on it—I had promised myself to wait until she did—and she was right here . . . (*Indicating.*) . . . turned away from me a little bit . . . but I could feel her pupils getting a little bigger as she's recognizing the thing in front of her . . . and she turns over, turns right to where I'm kneeling on the comforter . . . and I smiled at her. Without a word. Just that one smile . . . as I put my bayonet in her throat. Put it in there a couple times. Real fast, like this. (*Indicates.*) So she couldn't speak. (*Beat.*) I watched her dying, on our bed there, as her mouth opened up a couple times, trying to say a word or two . . . *something* . . . but she never got that far. There was just this whistling sound coming out. Through the holes I'd made. In her neck. (*Beat.*) And after that I loaded up and headed over to the Mess Hall and did what I did. To whoever was there. (*Waits.*) *He* was, wasn't he? With a bunch of those other assholes from "D" Company . . . I made sure I got to him first and the rest . . . well . . . that just happened. And I'm sorry about that. (*Beat.*) Like I said before . . . they teach you this shit and then they expect you can just switch it on and off. (*Claps his hands.*) BAM!!! Just like that. But you can't. It's not that easy . . . women can, maybe. Because of their powers. But not us . . . not guys . . . or at least not me. (*Beat.*) I mean . . . you people are *so* angry about what's happened and were yelling in my face before—"*Why'd* you do this?! *Why'd* you do this?!"—but hey . . . maybe you shouldn't've gone and showed me how to kill so good in the first place. Hmmmm? You ever think about that?

He stops for a moment. Collects himself. Looking straight ahead.

I don't have any special powers. Or stuff like that. I don't. I hear voices once in a while, or maybe it's just the wind. I'm not sure.

Doesn't matter. (*Beat.*) Anyway, you guys will do what you've gotta do . . . just like I did. That's the point and I'm sure you understand it, whether you wanna tell me you do or not. You know it's true. I had to do what I did. She did what she had to do and that motherfucker from my outfit, he did what he had to do, too. That's the way life works. You do what you gotta do. You do it because you want to or need to or for no damn reason at all. Sometimes you get away with it and life goes on . . . and sometimes you don't. You get hit by a car or used for target practice while you're walking down some dusty street in a place called "Kandahar." We live in a random fucking time and we just keep on spinning the wheel and throwing the dice and we shouldn't be surprised when our turn is up. But we are. We always are. (*Beat.*) I could see it in her eyes . . . she was very surprised. So were the guys over there . . . across the street . . . when I walked inside and they were laughing and eating their goddamn *omelets* . . . they were very fucking surprised, too . . . for about two seconds . . . and then they were dead and it didn't really matter whether they were surprised or not. (*Beat.*) And when time comes for me . . . when you do what you have to do, what I *know* you'll do . . . I guess I might be surprised as well. That it's my turn now . . . that it's finally here . . . but I really shouldn't be. Should I? (*Beat.*) No. I really shouldn't be at all . . .

He looks out into the light again. Smiles. Nods at this.

Well, who knows? Maybe I will be or maybe I won't. (*Beat.*) I guess we'll just have to wait and see . . .

The MAN *puts his head down now. Away from the light. He begins to drum his fingers on the table. To a beat that only he can hear.*

Silence. Darkness.

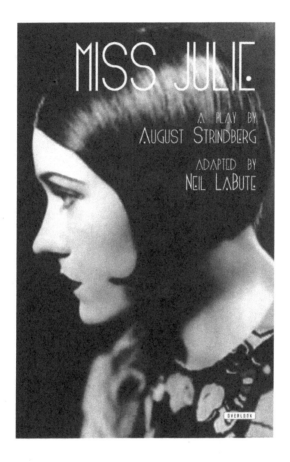

Set on Long Island just before the 1929 stock market crash and featuring one of theater's most commanding female characters, Neil LaBute's electrifying new adaptation of Strindberg's *Miss Julie* captures the timeless consequences of power, sex, and manipulation as servant and mistress of the house face off in a gripping night-long encounter. Commissioned for the 2012-13 season by the Geffen Playhouse.

"[Strindberg] has much to tell us of value . . . LaBute, as his distant descendant, understands this."   —**Myron Meisel, *The Hollywood Reporter***

$14.95   978-1-4683-0738-2

"mr. labute is writing some of the freshest and most illuminating dialogue to be heard anywhere these days." —ben brantley, *the new york times*

Things We Said Today
short plays & monologues by neil labute

OVERLOOK DUCKWORTH

Things We Said Today features the scripts for Neil LaBute's groundbreaking DirecTV project *Ten x Ten*—a series of short films written and directed by LaBute based on ten compelling original monologues, five each for men and women.

Also included are five short plays displaying the power and scope of LaBute's creative vision. In *Pick One*, written for the "Theatre Uncut" project and addressing the question "Do we get more 'right wing' in hard times?", three white guys come up with a way to solve America's problems. In *The Possible*, one young woman seduces another's boyfriend for an unexpected reason. *Call Back* features an actress and actor who spar about a past encounter that she remembers much better than he does. *Good Luck (In Farsi)*, "a pleasingly astringent study in competitiveness and vanity" *(The New York Times)* has two actresses pulling out all the stops in a pre-audition psych out; and in *Squeeze Play* a father and his son's baseball coach strike a mutually beneficial deal.

Rounding out the collection are two monologues from Center Stage Theatre's "My America" project.

$16.95 978-1-58567-0977-5

In the companion piece to Neil LaBute's 2009 Tony-nominated *Reasons to be Pretty*, Greg, Steph, Carly, and Kent pick up their lives three years later, but in different romantic pairings, as they each search desperately for that elusive object of desire: happiness.

"Mr. LaBute is more relaxed as a playwright than he's ever been. He is clearly having a good time revisiting old friends . . . you're likely to feel the same way . . . the most winning romantic comedy of the summer, replete with love talk, LaBute-style, which isn't so far from hate talk . . ." **—Ben Brantley, *The New York Times***

$14.95 978-1-4683-0721-4